THE TIN WHISTLE BOOK

by Tom Maguire

OSSIAN

D0176919

For a catalogue of all our publications and distributed items of
Irish and other music please send your name and address to:
OSSIAN PUBLICATIONS
14-15 Berners Street, London W1T 3LJ, UK.

Published by
OSSIAN PUBLICATIONS
14-15 Berners Street, London W1T 3LJ, UK.

Exclusive distributors:
MUSIC SALES LIMITED
Distribution Centre, Newmarket Road,
Bury St Edmunds, Suffolk, IP33 3YB, UK.

MUSIC SALES CORPORATION
257 Park Avenue South, New York, NY10010
United States Of America.

MUSIC SALES PTY LIMITED
120 Rothschild Avenue, Rosebery,
NSW 2018, Australia.

OMB29
ISBN 978-0-94600-525-3
This book © Copyright 2007 by Novello & Company Limited,
part of The Music Sales Group.

Printed in the EU.

www.musicsales.com

INTRODUCTION

Ever since the American, Irish and British folk revival of the 1950s and 60s, many instruments that were formerly regarded as not being ancient enough to be truly traditional have gradually been accepted into the mainstream of traditional music in many countries. Instruments such as the button and piano accordion, bouzouki/mandola, mouth-organ and guitar are today part and parcel of the instrumentation of much of our traditional music. In essence, the very high standard achieved by many musicians on these instruments has caused even the die-hard purists to realise that the instrument used is often secondary in importance to the quality of the performance.

The tin (or penny) whistle as we know it today stems from a long line of whistle-type ancestors known as aerophones. Right through the ages these whistle flutes have been used. Specimens have been found made of bone, clay, wood, cane or metal. Common characteristics of these whistle flutes are their mainly cylindrical construction, the air is directed through a simple mouthpiece against the sharp edge of a hole cut in the pipe just below the mouthpiece. (Finger holes or some other means of sounding different notes distinguish the whistle flute from the simple whistle)

early 13th century bone whistle, found
during excavations in Dublin 1968.

For a long time, whistles were sold as 'flageolets', which were really a rather more elaborate instrument, often handsomely decorated and used for art music in England and France from the 17th to the 19th century. For many years the tin whistle was considered a mere toy, to be found in the Christmas stocking or a birthday present, perhaps. They were sold at hardware stores, toy shops and by travelling hawkers, who incidentally may have been some of the very few, who in order to coax their young customers, actually could play familiar tunes on the whistle.

Most of the rolled tin whistles with their wooden underlip were first produced in the 19th century and this archetypal whistle is still made today. Around the turn of the century, a more durable instrument was made in England, France, and America, by using seamless brass tubing, a process still used today. Eventually manufacturers began to use plastic extrusions to shape the mouthpiece and gave the option of nickel plated or plain brass tubing. Although seemingly an easy item to mass produce, much care goes into the punching of the holes, lacquering and finishing of the whistle, while most importantly, care must be taken to ensure that the pitch is exactly as indicated. Available in the keys of Bb, C, D, Eb, F and G, the most commonly used are C and D.

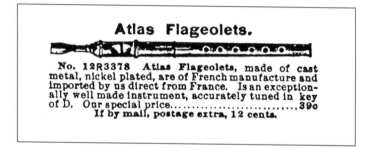

Atlas Flageolets.

No. 12R3378 Atlas Flageolets, made of cast metal, nickel plated, are of French manufacture and imported by us direct from France. Is an exceptionally well made instrument, accurately tuned in key of D. Our special price............................39c
If by mail, postage extra, 12 cents.

The playing of Irish musicians such as Willie Clancy, Micho Russell, Mary Bergin, Paddy Moloney and others has established the tin whistle as an instrument in its own right, capable of many traditional forms of music. Even outside the Irish/British/American musical sphere more and more musicians from all over Europe are now carrying the familiar 'whip it out and play it' whistle and use it to great effect in their own traditional music.

Tom Maguire

FIRST NOTES

HOW TO HOLD THE WHISTLE AND BLOW IT

Before we start, let's be absolutely sure that your whistle is in the key of D. It's the one that's needed for this particular book! Let's start off with an easy note, for which only one finger is needed, covering the hole closest to the mouthpiece. This is done with the index finger of the

left hand. The thumb of the same hand is supporting the underside of the barrel, directly underneath the first hole. Make sure that the index finger and thumb have a relaxed but firm hold on the whistle, without gripping it too tightly. The soft pad of the index finger is used to seal off the first hole effectively. As is shown, the finger is held at a fairly straight angle – this is important as eventually this will be useful in playing tunes at a reasonable speed.

Next, blow into the mouthpiece, just loud enough to get a steady, mellow sound. Blowing too softly will sound like 'the kettle's boiling' while blowing too hard will sound shrill and high pitched. Keep up a steady flow of air until that nice, soft, full tone is reached. The note produced by covering the first hole only is called **B**.

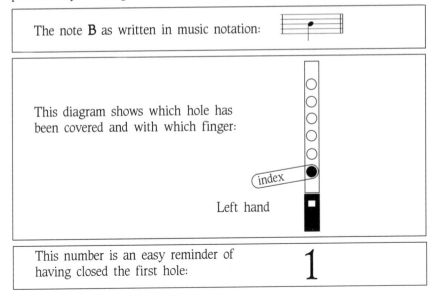

The note **B** as written in music notation:

This diagram shows which hole has been covered and with which finger:

index

Left hand

This number is an easy reminder of having closed the first hole: **1**

Now let's add another note and go down one step of the **scale** (from *scala:* Italian for ladder) by putting the middle finger down on the second hole.

This note is called **A:**   The third note is **G:**

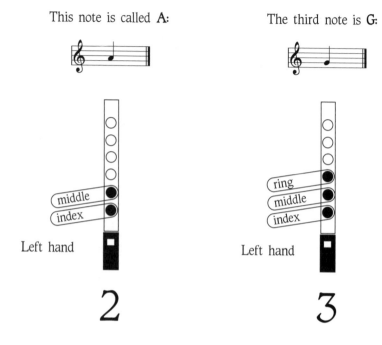

Try to play these first three notes, going up and down the scale and memorize their names and where to find them.

Tongueing

So far, you have probably kept up a constant airstream and have blown all these notes without pausing too much. The music may be played in this continuous way, or alternatively, with clear breaks between notes. Even the same note may be repeated several times and all notes will sound 'separately'. To get a clean start and finish to each note, make a 'tuh' sound in the mouth by bringing the tongue slightly against the upper teeth. In the following example, all notes are to be sounded in this way – known as tongueing.

Tongueing is used also to accentuate certain notes. If used throughout a piece however, it can sound a little tedious. Quite often it sounds good to have the first of a group of notes tongued to produce a nice smooth flow in a musical phrase.

Let's continue down the ladder and add another finger; this time the index finger of the right hand is put down on the 4th hole – while the right hand thumb is put under the barrel to support it – as we did before with the left hand. This note is **F**♯ (the ♯ stands for sharp).

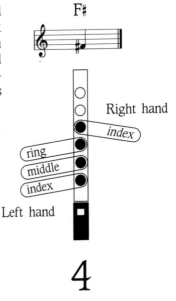

7

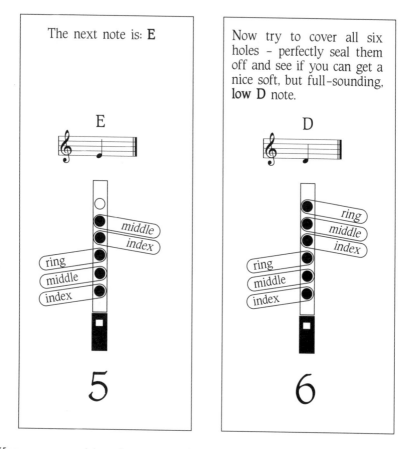

The next note is: **E**

E

Now try to cover all six holes - perfectly seal them off and see if you can get a nice soft, but full-sounding, **low D** note.

D

5

6

Keep on memorising the notes and where to find them. Here's a little exercise which may be tried both with continuous blowing or tongueing.

D F♯ A B E G F♯ E D B A F♯ E E D
6 4 2 1 5 3 4 5 6 1 2 4 5 5 6

Reading Music

We'll have to use a small bit of basic music reading at this stage, which, although it may look off-putting, will give you a sound foundation. Eventually this will enable you to enjoy the thrill of opening up any book of tunes and play them - as if a new language had been learnt. If you have never read music before, all the squiggly little bits look pretty confusing - Have no fear ! - We'll get through all this by breaking it down into basic elements.

The five lines on which the notes are written are called a **stave.** Notes are written resting on the lines and in the spaces between the lines. Consider the lines as the steps in a ladder - going up will make the whistle go higher in pitch - going down will sound lower.

This sign is called a **Treble Clef** and is used for most melody-instruments. In fact, most song and tune books will feature this symbol at the beginning of the stave.

If we choose a well-known tune like 'Twinkle-Twinkle', I'm certain that you will play some notes longer than others quite automatically. Having sung it and heard it so often takes care of that. Let's sing it now and look at this rhythm business: Most syllables are getting what's known as a beat (you may tap your foot along with each beat).

TWIN - KLE TWIN - KLE   LIT   - TLE   STAR-------

HOW   I   WON - DER   WHAT   YOU   ARE--------

However, did you notice how STAR and ARE became twice as long as the other words and syllables ? These are notes of longer duration and in the written music are given an extra beat - while the sound is held on - it looks like this:

9

As you can see, the music is broken up in smaller units, known as bars, with four beats in every bar.

The black notes ♩ receive one beat, the white notes ♩ get two beats.

Back to the whistle now – Try to play this first part of 'Twinkle Twinkle' and don't forget to keep on tapping, for convenience sake let's say a tap every second. The long 'STAR' and 'ARE' notes receive two taps and are held on during these two beats. Let's try the whole tune now:

TWINKLE TWINKLE LITTLE STAR

6 6 2 2   1 1 2   3 3 4 4   5 5 6

2 2 3 3   4 4 5   2 2 3 3   4 4 5

6 6 2 2   1 1 2   3 3 4 4   5 5 6

Notice how two numbers have appeared after the clef: The bottom one tells us the basic unit of notes are quarter notes (or crochets). The top number indicates how many of these are in each bar – in this case there are four quarter notes in each bar. Remember, the white ones count for two !

Try 'Twinkle Twinkle' again and this time tongue the first and third beat only in each bar. Rhythm is not the same as speed – the black and white notes only tell us about the length of time these notes are sounded in relation to each other. Of course 'Twinkle' could be played at breakneck speed or very slowly. This doesn't change the importance of the rhythm and beats.

ANOTHER TUNE

Ready for another tune? Frere Jacques is also in $\frac{4}{4}$ timing – four beats (taps) in a bar.

Sing it at first and find how at 'Sonnez les Matines' (Morning bells are ringing) the syllables sound much quicker compared to the other notes.

These are eighth notes (or quavers) and look like the usual black notes but with a little flag at the top when they're single ♪ or like this ♫ when together.

The white notes ♩ are half notes (or **minims**) and last twice as long as the black ones.

FRERE JACQUES

Are you sleeping, Are you sleeping,
Brother John, Brother John,
Morning Bells are ringing,
Morning bells are ringing,
Ding, ding dong, Ding ding dong.

Now that your repertoire has grown to two pieces, let's have another look at the notes we've learned so far. Start with the lowest sounding one and work your way up.

To continue the scale and complete the notes in the key of D we're going to add two new notes: First C♯. This is a bit of a balancing act: there are no fingers covering the holes, keep your thumbs at the usual places and let the fingers hover over their respective holes.

We'll finish with another D note, very similar in type of sound to the low D we know already. This one is a high D – called an octave higher (octave for 8th, as it is exactly eight notes from low to high D). To get this high D – cover all the holes except the first one. Now blow slightly harder than you normally would. Check the steps of your scale now by moving up from low to high D and make sure that the high D really is one step above C♯. This will take some practice but you'll succeed.

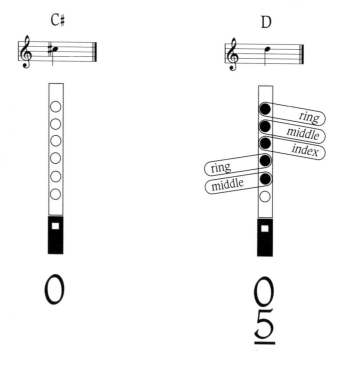

The names of the notes are the first seven letters of the alphabet, so that after the note G, another A is found. Like our low and high D's, the other notes too have high and low sounding relatives in other octaves.

The Key of D:
from low to high D

MORE TUNES & TRICKS

Here are some more easy tunes. First 'Jingle Bells', introducing a new note value: **o** a whole note (or semibreve) lasts for four beats. Rather than putting a ♯ (sharp) in front of every F and C note (which are automatically sharpened on the D whistle anyway) we will now write this into the **key signature.**

Every time we see these two sharps at the start of a tune, we know that the key of D is in force and **all C's and F's** throughout the tune are sharp, just as we've learned these two notes.

JINGLE BELLS

For 'London Bridge', notice the last note at the very end – the dot after the white note adds another half of its own value to its total length so that it lasts for 3 beats.

LONDON BRIDGE

2 1 2 3   4 3 2   5 4 3   4 3 2

2 1 2 3   4 3 2   5   2   4   6

The key of D as we learned has two sharps – F and C. A good many tunes can be played in other keys besides D, in fact often tunes are more or less stuck in a certain key, using certain notes and will simply have to be played like that. By removing the sharp from our C♯ and now calling it just C (or C natural) we can now play even more tunes in different keys.

Now play C♯ and C natural and notice the difference It's a half-step really (also known as a semitone).

C

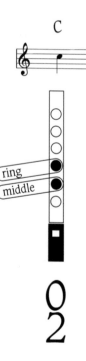

ring
middle

14

The C we just learned, together with all the notes we know already, enables us to play the following tune which is in the key of G, with only one sharp showing in the key signature.

IN DUBLIN'S FAIR CITY (COCKLES AND MUSSELS)

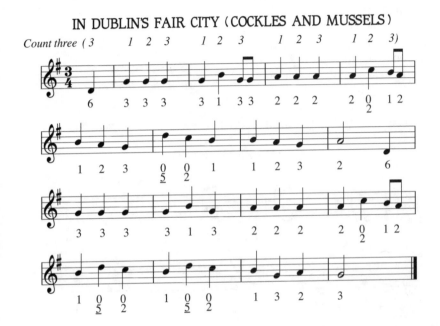

In the next tune 'Amazing Grace' you'll find a few new things:

This is a triplet, all three notes only last one beat together

Apart from tongueing we may also play notes in a smooth, flowing fashion; any time a **slur** appears, it connects the notes. This means that a smooth transition from one note to the next is required. There are no set rules that dictate when to use tongueing or **legato** (playing with slurs). Generally speaking a slow air doesn't need the type of punctuation that tongueing would bring to it. The best thing is to try each piece in different ways and get inspiration and ideas from other players and recordings.

TIES

It's easy to confuse a legato sign with a tie sign. They look alike, but a tie is only used to show that one note is to last longer (e.g. from one bar into the next). In this case the note is only blown once!

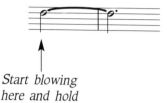

*Start blowing
here and hold*

The next tune will give you an opportunity to try our triplets and ties.

AMAZING GRACE

As you may have spotted, the last bar in some tunes doesn't make good counting sense, but you'll find the missing part at the start of the music. This happens often in songs, so that the song can be started up again, from the top, for the second verse.

LAST NOTES AND MORE TUNES

Here are some more notes in the higher octave, which will complete your range and will give you access to many hundreds of tunes. Remember to blow slightly harder for these notes.

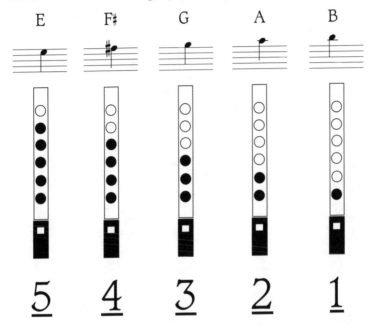

Seaġaŉ· ṁac Caṫṁaoıl· del.

The next traditional tune 'Scarborough Fair', although basically using the notes of the key of G, is really in a **minor key** which explains the lovely melancholy sound of this tune. There's no need to worry about the single C♯ in the tune, as we know that on this D whistle all the C's are automatically sharpened). Instead, concentrate on getting the C natural in the second bar to sound correct. Notice also that in the key signature only one sharp appears. Go slowly and check back to the note charts if you feel it doesn't sound right.

SCARBOROUGH FAIR

Breath Control

An essential part in your vocabulary; a nice even flow and a sense of when to take a breath between the notes are very important. No hard or fast rules exist here - each player tackles it differently. Especially in dance music you'll have to feel the length of a phrase and quickly breathe in between two phrases. Practice makes perfect!

The following rhythms are commonly found in traditional tunes:

2/4   2 beats in a bar   Hornpipes, marches, polkas, reels and break-downs.

3/4   3 beats in a bar   Slow airs, songs, waltzes

4/4   4 beats in a bar   Polkas, marches, reels, hornpipes, set dances, old time

6/8   6 quavers   Double jigs, set tunes (2 beat feel)

9/8   9 quavers   Slip jigs (3 beat feel)

12/8   12 quavers   Slides, single jigs (4 beat feel)

stands for four sixteenth notes (semiquavers) equalling in duration one quarter note (crotchet).

is a **rest** (no sound) for the length of a ♪. Remember the slurs – for smooth playing - and the ties for connecting the notes together!

Dotted eighth notes. 2 eighth notes (quavers): 1½ plus ½, making a total of one quarter note in length (one crotchet). This is often used in songs, reels and hornpipes.

Triplets. 3 notes played in the time of one quarter note ♩ (crotchet). To get the feel of these dotted notes and triplets try to sing this and then play:

Hump - ty Dump - ty   sat   on   the   wall
1   2   3   4

In some pieces use is made of the 'Scotch Snap' in which the first note is the quick one.

JIGGITY RHYTHMS AND OTHER THINGS

Here are some examples of tune types with different rhythms.

6   6 eighths (quavers) in a bar. Usually these 6 notes: ♪ ♪ ♪ ♪ ♪ ♪
8   are grouped together in two groups of three to show the rhythm.
(Look at the butter and sausages below!)

A dotted quarter note ♩. equals ♪ ♪ ♪

Try out this new rhythm using the late Seán O Riada's method for explaining where the notes ought to be stressed. Tap twice for every bar and say the words.

Ham and eggs and   but-ter and sau-sa-ges,   Ham and cof-fee and   bread with cheese
 1   2   1   2   1   2   1   2

Although there are 6 eighth notes to make up each bar, in reality there should be a sustained two-feel. Try tapping at the marked notes and put some stress on the first and fourth quaver positions.

Hum the next song first a few times and try to get this 'two' feel, then play it.

HERE WE GO GATHERING NUTS IN MAY

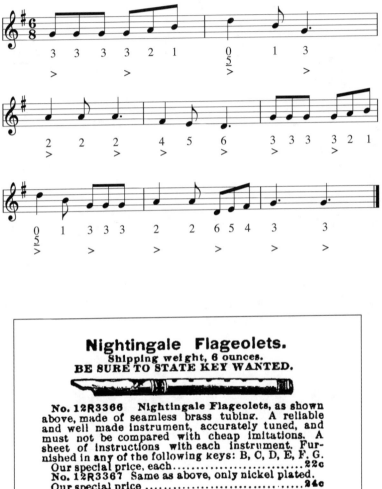

Next, we'll try to combine everthing we've learned so far, including; the new high notes of E, F♯, G, A and B. Also the practising of the $\frac{6}{8}$ rhythm should come in handy now as we attempt, quite slowly, but in strict time, the following well known Irish jig:

THE IRISH WASHERWOMAN

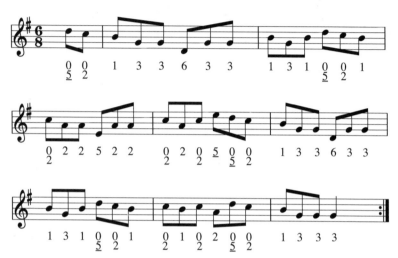

```
0   0   1   3   3   6   3   3       1   3   1   0   0   1
5   2                                           5   2
```

```
0   2   2   5   2   2       0   2   0   5   0   0       1   3   3   6   3   3
2                           2       2   5   2
```

```
1   3   1   0   0   1       0   1   0   2   0   0       1   3   3   3
        5   2               2       2   5   2
```

The ⫶‖ sign at the end means **repeat** this section, so go back to the very beginning and play it a second time.

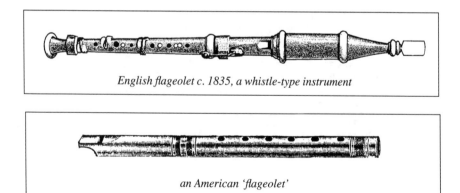

English flageolet c. 1835, a whistle-type instrument

an American 'flageolet'

So far so good, apart from the Jig-gi-ty, Jig-gi-ty rhythm and the high E in the fifth bar there are not too many difficulties here. Now grit your teeth for the second part which, as is usual with this type of tune uses a lot of the higher octave notes.

Once again this section is repeated, after which you are free to stop or to start again with the first part.

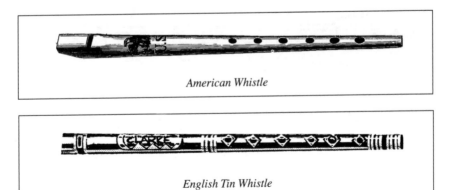

American Whistle

English Tin Whistle

C amptown Races' is in 2/4 timing: two quarter notes to a bar. Be careful
at the last bar of the first line and the first of the second line, where
first the F ♯ is <u>slurred</u> into an E note and then <u>tied</u> to another E,

CAMPTOWN RACES

Here are some musical signs and symbols you may encounter in this and other books: ♮ the **natural** restores a sharpened note to its original pitch: Unless this sign appears again, in the next bar and the rest of the tune all the C's are to be as indicated in the key signature (sharp in this case).

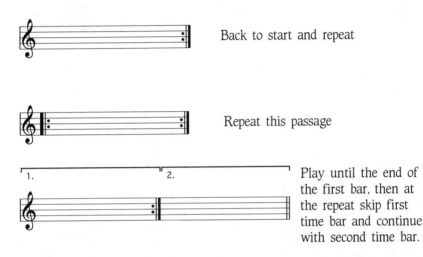

Back to start and repeat

Repeat this passage

Play until the end of the first bar, then at the repeat skip first time bar and continue with second time bar.

D.C. (Da Capo) back to the very start and play until **Fine** (end).

٧ Rest (silence) equals: ♪

Σ Rest (silence) equals: ♩

— Rest (silence) equals: ♩

⌒ Pause

Notes may appear in different groupings and combinations but the total value of all the notes in one bar always adds up to the value stated in the time signature at the start of the tune.

ORNAMENTATION

All traditional musicians use various forms of ornamentation, many of these forms depend on the instrument used. There are many ways to embellish a tune on the tin whistle. Common ones such as the **Cut** are much like the 'grace notes' used in classical music.

Example:

The small G grace note is thrown into the main F ♯, so that although it has little time value of its own, it creates a nice effect.

Geraldine Cotter's **Traditional Irish Tin Whistle Tutor** (also Published by Ossian Publications) would be suitable for more study in this field of articulation and decoration of traditional tunes. Cuts, rolls, casadh, etc, are all discussed in this book.

These are all the notes learned:

With these notes and all you have learned about rhythm and reading music we're ready to progress and play from a selection of traditional tunes and song airs from many countries.

TO EXPAND YOUR MUSICAL HORIZONS . . .

Here are some more titles of books and recordings, which will help you with further study of the whistle:

AN IRISH WHISTLE TUNE BOOK by Tom Maguire
42 of the finest old Irish Song-Airs and a selection of lively traditional dance tunes: Reels, Jigs, Hornpipes, Slides, Polkas etc. All tunes are also suitable for most other traditional instruments. 40 pages. Ossian OMB 106
Also available: TUNES RECORDING: All 42 tunes from the book are here played out fully with repeats in 'medley' sets by 'Hammy' Hamilton and friends. Apart from accompanying the book it is also a unique musical treat in its own right! Book + CD OMB 7, CD alone OSSCD 122

TRADITIONAL IRISH TIN WHISTLE TUTOR by Geraldine Cotter
A complete method for the Irish tin whistle with an appendix of 100 choice Irish airs and dance tunes. Although suitable for beginners, this book presents a comprehensive and advanced course, with particular emphasis on Irish music in all its forms. OMB 31
DEMO RECORDING
All techniques discussed in the book played out in full.
CD: OSSCD 35
TUNES RECORDING
All 100 tunes from the final section of the book.
Each tune is played without repeats.
Double CD: OSSCD 107

TOTALLY TRADITIONAL TIN WHISTLES
If you ever wondered what can be done with a modest little instrument such as the tin whistle-here's your chance ! 16 tracks by ace players: Willie Clancy, Miko Russell, Fintan Vallely, Josie McDermott, Michael Tubridy and Cathal McConnell.   CD: OSSCD 53

TRADITIONAL SONG & DANCE TUNES FROM MANY LANDS

song

TAE THE WEAVERS GIN YE GO

Scottish

jig

HE PIPED SO SWEET

Scottish

children's song

SKINNY MALINKY LANGLEGS

Scottish

reel

ROLL HER ON THE HILL

Scottish

song

CAM' YE O'ER FRAE FRANCE

Scottish

jig

THE MONAGHAN JIG

Irish

march 'MORE' OF CLOYNE Irish

double jig THE DANCING MASTER Irish

quadrille PADDY DOYLE Irish

harptune by O'Carolan

SI BEAG, SI MOR

Irish

air

SLIABH NA MBAN

Irish

polka

EGAN'S POLKA

Irish

reel

THE FLAX IN BLOOM

Irish

slide

A KERRY SLIDE

Irish

hornpipe — **A HORNPIPE** — Irish

jig — **WE MUST ALL WAIT TILL MY LADY COMES HOME** — English

morris dance — **THE GIRL I LEFT BEHIND ME** — English

35

reel · THE TIDE COME IN · English

morris dance/song · ENGLISH COUNTRY GARDEN · English

country dance · MORRIS MARCH · English

song

VIVE LA CANADIENNE

Canadian

song

EN ROULANT MA BOULE

Canadian

reel

RONFLEUSE GOBEIL

Canadian

song   **PRETTY SARO**   American

reel   **NIMBLE FINGERS**   American

Fine

D.C.

waltz   **FROM FRISCO TO CAPE COD**   American

38

jig   **LADY IN THE BOAT**   American

hymn   **SHALL WE GATHER AT THE RIVER**   American

old time   **JAYBIRD**   American

39

march
THE YEAR OF THE JUBALO
American

song & jig
HELA'R SGYFARNOG
Welsh

song
Y GELYNEN
Welsh

18th cent. harptune   **LADY OWEN'S DELIGHT**   Welsh

hornpipe   **THE SWANSEA HORNPIPE**   Welsh

song/dance air   **LE PONT DE MORLAIX**   Breton

song

MA FRANZEZ

Breton

song

AR BARADOZ

Breton

song

ME ANVEZ EUR GOULMIK

Breton

polka

THE HEEL AND TOE POLKA

Australian

song

THE POMMY'S LAMENT

Australian

dance tune THE SYDNEY FLASH Australian

song CLICK GO THE SHEARS BOYS Australian

Would you like to take your whistle-playing a step further ?

TRADITIONAL IRISH TIN WHISTLE TUTOR

by Geraldine Cotter - A complete method for the Irish tin whistle with an appendix of 100 choice Irish airs and dance tunes. The standard book ! 104 pages. OMB 31, ISBN 0 946005 12 5

Accompanying Demo CD's of the tutorial and tune parts are available

Note	English name	North American Name	Equivalent Rest
♪	Semiquaver	Sixteenth note	𝄿
♪	Quaver	Eight note	𝄾
♩	Crotchet	Quarter note	𝄽
𝅗	Minim	Half note	▬
o	Semibreve	Whole note	▬

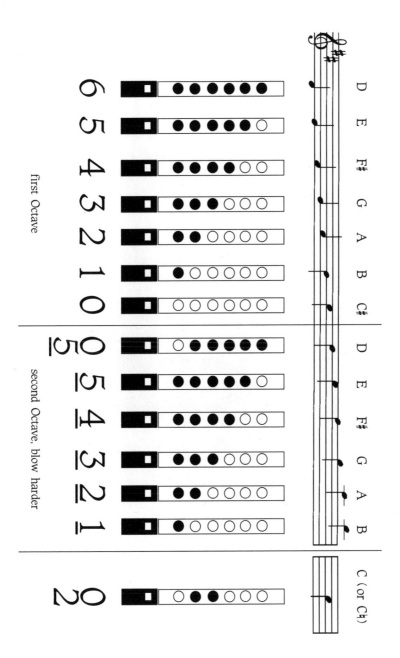